PLEASE, TAKE PHOTOGRAPHS

modjaji books

PLEASE, TAKE PHOTOGRAPHS

 SINDIWE MAGONA

Publication © Modjaji Books 2009
Text © Sindiwe Magona 2009

First published in 2009 by Modjaji Books CC
P O Box 385, Athlone, 7760, South Africa
modjaji.books@gmail.com
http://modjaji.book.co.za

ISBN 978-0-9802729-5-6

Editing: Angela du Preez
Book and cover design: Natascha Mostert
Lettering: Hannah Morris

Printed and bound by Harbec Packaging, Cape Town
Set in Palatino 11/14 pt

Cape Tercentenary Foundation

In fond memory of "Ta Mri" Mawethu, my brother, who taught me so much about the profundity of silence

Contents

Across the River Kei

Land of low skies, far horizons;
Sunrises that glow low steeples,
Paint cow horns above still
Far-from-discernible bodies
Huddled close in the morning kraal,
Chewing yesterday's cud as sun's early rays
Listen to the satisfied moos of cows
All heralding the dawn; early sun
Buttering morning clouds,
Bidding lovers disengage.

Buried treasure

Here lies, buried, precious treasure
The future of our beloved land
Pride of our fledgling nation
Our youth, our joy, our hope,
Now turned to sorrowing dust.

They were all young, but children, really
In the full flush of youth
Such promise for the hungry tomorrow
Blessings betrayed and all rules
Of nature turned upside down.

The girls gaily giggled
The young men, boys, really,
Whistled and winked as they strutted about
It was all such fun, such youthful fun
The words of parents paled beside.

The words of parents, mostly whispered;
And even that by but a few.
A whole nation looked on, but shirked duty
As the future swiftly withered and died.

They were in school, but the teachers taught nothing.
Some went to church, but the priests spoke little about daily
    living;
Pie in the sky and peace and bliss hereafter, their only
    platform.

Gone, too, the wisdom of the Old
Forsaken, the knowledge of yesteryear
That knew and accepted what is only natural

Understood the folly that would block the swells of a
   surging river
And knew how all children needed mothers and fathers;
Embraced all children; charged every man and woman with
   their nurturing.

'It takes a village', belatedly, we now say; at last
   remembering
Faded lessons, traditions hastily discarded in blind pursuit
Of progress, of fashion, of assimilation. Now, finally seeing
How we ran open-armed, embracing our annihilation.
Now, sorrow jogs memory and we join empty hands
As we frantically try once more to guide,
To lead the new generation as before,
To show the way to the House of Adulthood
Leaving none behind, losing few as can be.

Eye turned back to a time long forgotten
When the measure of a man
Was not the fatness of his pocket
But his deeds of glory; shunning abomination.
When neighbour trusted neighbour; his safety secure at his
   presence
His home, his folk, his property – all sovereign
His neighbour, his best protection against all
His children, insurance against old age and infirmity.
But that was before the nation learnt to bury all its children;
See its morrow fade, its treasure interred;
The youth, its pride, its hope and joy obliterated.
The nation's tomorrow, no more – ah, sad day,
When we buried our most precious treasures!

It takes a village

It takes a village
To raise a child
Mother to tomorrow's
Village.

It takes a village
To heal broken accord
Child to tomorrow's
War.

It takes a village
To plough the widow's field
So her children will not steal
To live.

It takes a village
To sow seeds of life
Cooperation, life-blood
To communal living.

It takes a village
To raise a standard,
Kill competition, father
Of greed and unending strife.

A rock

I am a rock
Sturdy and strong.
I am a rock
Damn hardy; do not forget.
Were it not so,
I wouldn't be here to tell the tale.

Don't pick on me. Don't be so damned astounded.
The cracks you see are battle scars, my friend.
Daily, I do battle.
Daily, I wage war.
Daily, I dodge and run and flinch and smile,
Deflecting blows.
Deflecting unthinking rained-upon-me blows;
And blows in the national psyche deep, deep ingrained.

And then you ask: Why do you bleed?

I am a rock
Sturdy and strong.
Were it not so,
I wouldn't be here to tell the tale.

Motherhood

Woman: Baby on back
Smile on her face
Why so intense, her gaze?

Woman: Baby on breast
Arms holding love
Why's fear gnawing at her heart?

Out in the yard; sun overhead,
Smiling little ones by her side
Busy shucking corn, all eager hands

Hands that never rest, from morn
Till midnight; cooking, washing,
Fetching, mending, and stilling troubled
                    Little hearts.

Life Song on sweet lip,
Warm love on swaying hip,
Honey-soft the touch of her hand.

This is the beginning; this is the end –
Carrier of Afrika's Seed; Nurturer of a
Continent's Tomorrow, Centre of its
                    Very survival.

In calm and in storm – unbowed,
Tall she stands. Afrika's Beacon
Motherhood is her name.

From *Windows To The Soul: Photographs celebrating African Women* by A. Olusegun Fayemi, Albofa Press, 2001

Being

Because it pleases our Maker
We have no choice
In the fashion of our making.
The sentence, for our being,
Is choice
In the manner of our living.

Writing

Writing is not therapy
But it could be therapeutic.
It is not magic
But should be magical.
It is not hell
Yet, often, is hellish.
Writing is not brutality
But can be brutal.
It is not real
But must be realistic
Which is why its flesh
And bones are the
Local and specific
To say something
Original and provocative
About the larger condition of
Frail humanity.

Imagination

Imagination is all the worlds that inhabit you
The worlds that have swallowed you
Since long before you were born.
The worlds all the mothers
And fathers of your race remember
That they have handed down through
The blood in your veins. It is the fire
That burns and scorches all; the ice
That freezes the very breath and leaves
All still. All – all still, deep in your core.
It is the thunder, the lightning, the hail,
And the tranquil song of a grain of sand.
It is the loud bang that shook,
And ceaselessly shakes, the world.
Timeless. Boundless. Beyond
All you can conceive;
Greater than the sum of
Your highest hopes.

For Maria

The first decade – I learnt to wipe my nose
Wipe my feet before entering the house
After a walk in the rain or on snow.

The second decade – I learned to put on lipstick
Look in the mirror before
Leaving the house
Look at a boy without letting him know
I was looking
Look like a lady without letting Mama know
I felt all womanish inside.

The third decade – I learned to wipe other people's noses
And love it
I learned to put another's interest before mine
Love and duty were but two sides of the same coin
Complain?
Me?
What did I have to complain about?
I was fulfilled! Grown up, married, with children and all,
A roof over my head. A boiling pot on the stove
And a man who told me, at least twice a day,
He worshipped the ground I walked on!
Yes, sometimes, very late at night, he reminded me
How much he loved me –
Very, very, very late at night; when the children were
Fast asleep.
When all the dishes were sparkling clean
When the floor was swept free of all toys,
Dusted, and wiped free of meddlesome footprints
Yes, sometimes, late at night, he reminded me
For the third time that day, how much

He loved me.

The fourth decade – I watched my own children,
My daughters, make goo-goo eyes at boys
When they thought my eyes were closed
My ears deaf as stone
They whispered tingly secrets; made subtly suggestive
Gestures. Amused, I watched it all – though, inside,
I sighed; amused to see the pattern repeat itself. Oh, my
   God!
Embarrassed, I remembered my own naïve assumption of
My mother's blindness.

The fifth decade – there was no denying it – my children
Were grown. Yes, they were *my* children; but they,
Definitely, were no longer children!
Did this mean I was old?
How could it be – when had that happened?
I was just discovering my essence!
Discovering joyful living *sans* fear of pregnancy,
Sin or ridicule! It was in such ecstatic sensuousness
I entered

The sixth decade – let no one misguide you,
The fifties are for fleshly fulfillment, sinful
Delight, and sprightly goings on. Now, at last,
I knew all there was to know about life.
I'd even made it, from scratch, myself
Gave it flesh, blood, and bone
Knit it and bled it into being,
Nurtured it to healthy maturity.

The seventh decade – I learned to live with loss
A huge hole came to live in my heart
But I learned to understand this:

The loss is as big as the love. I suffer
Greatly for I have greatly loved
I am grateful for the love that was mine.
I suffer, but I could not have asked for less.

The eighth decade – I learned to live with
Fewer and fewer friends
Fewer and fewer visits from my children
As their own lives grew fuller and fuller

I love the four walls I call home
I love the skin that houses the bones I call my body
I love the people who, a long time ago,
Were my children
I look at their clean noses and know
I have lived a good life. Look. Just look!
How they truly no longer need me!

The ninth decade – I will learn the meaning of hours
For time is short, each hour more precious, therefore!
The journey is definitely longer behind me
The road ahead looks short indeed
But, my heart lifts with joy as I see
Footsteps painted a bright and
Joyful gold!
Without a doubt, I know, those are the footsteps
Love has made.
Mine has been a long life – rich in experience.

But now, looking back, I see all those brilliant
Moments in my life are moments of loving,
Of giving to others. These are moments
When I transcended the self and its
Imperious demands. When I was for
Another – whatever it was they needed

To go one step forward: wife; friend;
Mother; neighbour; daughter; sister; or
Stranger!

Yes, I can see: I have been a good citizen, a decent
Human being.
Now, I am eighty years old – I hope I still have
Time enough to catch up!
Pass me that damn bottle of wine, will you?

They brought light

To bring light
Far they came, and
Naught they saw
In all they surveyed.

The other,
Candidates
For salvation.
Alive. Well. With their
Ways of doing things.
Alive. Well.
Birthing and marrying and
Feasting and worshipping
Their gods.
Hunting. Building. And
Healing their ill.

To bring light
They came and
Naught they saw
But indolence, ignorance and
Superstition, rife and rude.

To bring light, they came.
Condemned all they surveyed.
The singing, the dancing,
The joy in living was
To their cold eye
Something to stamp out
Something to kill. Ruthlessly
To exterminate.

Great is the white man!

Great is the white man!
Said our fathers,
Pushing *iingolovane*
Bodies steamy with sweat.

Absent the mothers
Left behind in the homeland
Alone to plough barren fields
Feet cracked hard by uncaring clods

Great is the white man
So said our fathers
Cooling boiling blood
Averting eye from war undeclared

Seeing ingrained deceit;
Opportunity denied.
What wondrous wisdom
To hail him you would kill!

Translated from Xhosa saying *Mdal' umlungu* (lit. Old is the
    white man, i.e. wise/great)

Fear of change

April, 1994
With bated breath, we wait;
At last, we join the rest of
Progressive humanity!
UHURU! INKULULEKO! KIKIKIKIKIKI!
Shall we sing and dance,
Our cup truly overflowing?

Why, then, am I not overjoyed,
Frozen my heart?
Shall I with you a secret share?

My biggest fear, what makes me
Tremble, fearing the terrific morrow:
I have seen the Promised Land –
Harlem, US of A!

The world has a memory
Swifter than a blink.
Give it a decade or two, if that;
Then fast and full will questions flow…

Why are they not making it?
What's holding them back, now?
After all, apartheid is gone!

I have seen the thick-welted scars
On people rudely plucked from hearth and
Home. Bound hand and bleeding foot;
Kicked, punched, raped, and ravaged
Every way you care to think.
Killed – in their millions and

Dumped on icy wave.

And today, those unlucky enough to
Survive the gruesome plunder,
Annoy the world by failing to be quite,
Quite human. By falling short of accepted
Standards of civilisation. Never mind that
On these people was performed a
National lobotomy that has left them with
No tongue of their own…
No tongue
To call
Their own!

The great learning

The silence of absence
Is a great teacher
I should know, for
I learned a lot from Tata,
Who was never there.

Married by law and
Before the eyes of God
White man's law dictated
Three weeks out of a year
Enough time to spend with family.

All through his working life
Condemned to Single Men's
Barracks; bug-infested quarters;
His hands all that was desired.
Brainless brawn, to hew and till.

Tata, your absence, a heavy silence
I grew up without solace
Fatherless, without role model
To knit my wits to manhood
No steps to follow, no man to shadow.

I am what I am through no fault
Of yours. I am what I am for
History deemed it. Your absence,
The silence, taught me only too
Well. I am what I am. Yes, I am!

Mine boys

An inconvenience now, the train ride seems;
Laughable almost, by present horror dimmed.
Black bodies gleaming, all in line,
A throng, a thousand strong.
Old and young alike, all bare of clothing.
Standing, gleaming, seemingly unbowed.
Naked as unpodded bean,
Alone, each man stands
His cover alone, his stifled feelings.
Forward, the line shuffles,
Men going for treatment.
Strong black bodies gleaming
Defenceless as defanged snakes.

In this new scene of initiation,
This bizarre manner of induction,
Each man is dusted;
With powder, cleansed and purified.
Risk of illness diminished
This is Company Policy:
Maximise Investment Potential!

The men are dusted,
Everywhere vermin lurked;
The men are dusted,
Everywhere vermin suspected:
On head.
Under arms.
Between legs.
One by one
The mine boys are dusted.
One by one

With sprayings of DDT.
And, coming up from down under,
Naked they stand for search:
Tawuza!
High, lift leg!
High! High!
Higher!
Push out! Push out!
PUSH OUT!
Show anus free of precious stones.
Show anus free of white man's germs.

Excerpt from *Penrose,* a biography of the author's father in verse.

The prize

For some it's easy
For others not so
For me it was
Very difficult, indeed.

But five years into wifehood
Belly flat as a starving bed bug's
Mother-in-law far from pleased
Your father and I were desperate.

The law stated: Three months!
Enough for wife's visitation
To get her belly pumped full
And return to birth child in village.

But for me, it had not happened
An extension, clearly, we needed
To the Pass Office, thus, we hastened
To beg the white man for more time.

White shirt, black tie, pink face
Slit-eyed, thin-lipped; he asked your father:
Do you eject Pepsi Cola into her vagina?
She's been here long enough!

What could we do but smile,
Treat insult as kindness or
Joke, at worst. What could tata do but
Beg for time?
And, there you are!

Men at the corner of the road

From morning till evening
They stand at the corners of nameless streets
Men with nowhere to go
Men running away from hunger at home
Men who cannot bear the sight
Of wives and children, belly extended,
Eyes widened; waiting for food
That never comes. Men with nowhere
To go, all day long. Men who wait for
Chance, someone who needs a pair of
Hands to do what the absent worker can't.
Men paid peanuts by ruthless exploiters
Who pick them up from the corners of roads
Where they huddle in hopes of being picked
Any day, by any one, for any thing
Men whose hopes have long been dashed
Men who live on the thin bread of 'Things are
So bad, they cannot but improve!'

Laugh not at their plight, you who still
Have a tomorrow; being so young
Still in school. Laugh not at their plight.
That is not the lesson, at all.
But, in grateful humility
Accept the gift of wasted life
Opportunities missed or unseen,
Unrecognised, unseized;
And shun it with all your might.

Victims of an undeclared war

In South Africa
Woman lives under threat
No less than if she
Were in a war-zone.

Embattled, daily, she rises
To face yet another day
Of uncertainty, fear, abuse
At the hands of men
Especially the men she loves.

Daily, she is raped
Daily she is robbed
Daily she is murdered
Daily she suffers humiliation
And abuse of one or another kind.

How long must she wait?
When will her freedom come?
Freedom to live free of fear;
To go about her business
Unhindered, unafraid?

World champions

My son,
My lover,
My father,
My neighbour,
My brother,
My friend,
My sworn foe,
My employer,
My President
My Ambassador,
My Member of Parliament,
My solicitor,
My butcher,
My greengrocer,
My taxi driver or
My taxi owner,
My teacher,
My spiritual leader,

Answer me! Please, answer me! If you are rape champions
  of the world, what is my name?

Community building

Lives there a woman
Who is not a
Community leader?

Lives there a mother
Who is not a
Teacher?

Lives there a girl
Or woman who has
Not suffered indignity?

At the hands of the
Other half of humanity,
Woman has suffered; has
Toiled unappreciated.

At the mercy of the
Lords she raises
Woman suffers rape
And worse. At the hands of
Princes professing undying love
She dies.

The time is now
The time has come
The army must rise
To save all humanity.

On the run

Inspired by the photographs of UN photographer John Isaac

Skin and bones
Wrinkled skin
But mostly bone
On she crawls
Snail's pace
She crawls
In search of water
In search of food
In search of safety
Warlords ejected her
From home and the familiar.

Mama Afrika runs for life
From her sons
From her brothers
From her father
Marauding hordes after her,
She flees.

What is this war
Men of Africa wage
On Africa's women?
On Africa's children?
And we don't call it by name!

The leader

Inspired by the photographs of UN photographer John Isaac

Rake thin, this old woman
At the head of a straggling line.
Eye fixed on distant horizon,
Strides along the famished road.
The corpses she'll feed it behind her;
Disciples going toward the Cross;
Pilate, the men Africa calls leaders.

What Africa needs

Africa needs teachers
Africa needs fathers
Africa needs mothers
Africa needs children
Africa needs doctors
Africa needs nurses
Africa needs farmers
Africa needs miners
Africa needs dancers
Africa needs filmmakers
Africa needs journalists
Africa needs builders
Africa needs welders
Africa needs surveyors
Africa needs bakers
Africa needs fishermen
Africa needs scientists
Africa needs architects
Africa needs photographers
Africa needs rulers
Africa needs singers
Africa needs storytellers

But, above all, Africa needs good, honest governments.
And what Africa does not need are killers! In all their
    manifold
Guises: greedy power-mongers; rapists; pimps; many-
    wived vainglorious
Men, brains residing below the navel.

All are precious

When we remember
That each one of us comes to this earth
A promise to the world
A bundle of great gifts, talents;
Then the question we must ask:
What gives us the right
To lay waste such bounty?

How dare we kill
Those gifts freely given?
How dare we deprive
The world of what
It sorely needs?

And then we have the nerve
To bewail our sad fate
When we steadfastly continue,
Willfully, to denude ourselves
Of the good God gives us.

Nothing is superfluous
The universe gives
According to Earth's needs
The very least of these
That we do not mind
Is robbery of the granary,
Seed of our own destruction.

Imperfect present

This shallow grave you see
Perhaps dug by the victim herself
When she knew she must lay herself down
And die in the ditch she'd dug with bare hands.

This was somebody's child, lest we forget.
In kinder climes, where rain came during
The rainy season; and cold settled scores
In winter; cleansed the land, rested the soil
And blooms lay in wait for spring
To awaken into gay and sprightly bloom
And ripen in bounteousness in the autumn
She would have lived to the summer of
Her life and, having given fruit aplenty,
Shed seed, reaffirming life.

Instead, this sad bundle of bones you see
Is all that remains of her; all she gives us!

On her blindness

Often, I think of how dark is my life
Deprived all day and night of light.
Then, curse I out loud the gods
For dealing me a fate so cruel:
Neither colour nor shape do I perceive;
A mole among the human race.
But then I hear of strife in schools
Reflection, no doubt, of attitudes abroad;
Cursing and shoving and boxing,
Kicking and even knifing. Or, worse still,
Shooting to kill! Then I see: How lucky,
How blessed, to escape the terrible curse;
Sight, gateway to another's slight; and
Perhaps hate to fill all my heart.

Apples

Ripe and ready; apples
At picking season.
But these were fathers,
Not apples, when
Younger women boasting
Fat, shiny cheeks
Sweet lips, plump thighs
Plucked them from home,
Easy as apples from the tree
Drop off into greedy basket
Without one backward glance, welcome
The picker's ensnaring hand.
Doesn't the apple ever look back
To the tree that gave it life
Sustained it through gale, frost
And drought – so that it got
The rosy cheek it boasts?
So that, full of juice, it now
Attracts the picker's lusting eye?

Our house is on fire

Our house is on fire; but the future is secure
If we will mind the young
If we will count each child
If the child who never saw her father
If a child in the little village
As well as the child in the big city
Will have a roof over her head
Food that supports health and growth
Schooling that ensures her becoming
Whatever she was meant to be.

Our house is on fire; but the future is secure
If each child will have enough adults
Knitting their hands together tightly
So she stands not a chance of seeing,
Never mind falling through, any
Crack. Then, our future is secure.
If the child in slum or town or city
Like the child in hamlet, village, or farm
Has time and space and freedom
To roam and wonder at nature
Busy unfolding beneath her very feet.

Our house is on fire; but if all the children are counted
If all are held precious, if they're helped unfold the gifts
They come to us bearing, if each child can laugh,
Each day, confident in the knowledge of
Her uncompromised childhood –
A precious seed busy unfolding, unfurling
As it should –
To bear fruit bountiful, at time of ripening;
Then, indeed, is our future secure.
Then, assuredly, shall the nation not perish.

Speak, bones!

Is that you, Danai?
Is that you, my friend?
Come in, come in.
Let me see you. Let me look at you,
For it's been a while.

Please, come closer
My eyesight fails, you know?
Come nearer, my friend, please do,
For my voice is but a whisper these days.

I see you start – the doctor says I've lost twenty kilos.
Should I believe him? – I don't feel that thin,
But your eyes tell me this may, indeed, be so.

Only last week, it seems,
Was I strong as an ox, my friend.
Up and about, frolicking like a lamb in spring.
When I heard I was ill, I was the last to believe
And the mirror, that wicked liar, confirmed
My suspicion: the stupid doctors erred.

Indeed, I thought the rogues in league with my wife
Who'd been at me to stop this, stop that,
All the things that tell a man he's alive,
That red-hot blood runs in his veins.
But what man's man pays heed to such fluff?

Poor dear, of all the luck. She, so pure of heart,
To end up dying of Aids when she didn't have
Half the fun – for that's what we thought it was,
Didn't we, old chap? Fun, when all the time

We were running, with open arms, to the grave.

Look at me now: wrinkled skin, dry bones
Reduced to wearing Pampers, like a babe in arms.
Except, of course – though only liquid and pulp
Keep these bones alive, all food too much for
My poor body to digest – (I, who used to eat raw meat,
Have a whole chicken for a snack, a loaf of bread
To accompany the miserable tidbit)
It is far from baby pooh, that out of me flows.
The stench, O my friend, knocks the socks off
My feet! Futile tears just add to the pain,
The embarrassment! I truly wish I were dead.

I said, when I heard you'd sent word,
Let him come, let him come –
So you could see and learn.
For if there's anything you should take
From this rubble, this bag of bones, so frail
A breath can blow it clean away, it's the horror:
He used to be a man, strong as an ox...
Remember that and go tell the world, beginning
With your dear self: Aids kills. It does not
Discriminate, equal opportunity, swift as the wind.
One and only one way is sure, only one –
Stay sure, by staying within a given range
Stock that graze far and wide, for sure, soon,
Will feed on poisoned grass:
Feed with no knowledge of doom;
The grass, sweet as before, no trace,
No trace of death in the blood.

I said you should come
Not that I am a spectacle or to be pitied
(How would that help me, now?)

But so I could mirror the folly of indiscretion
And you, bear witness and henceforth shun
Behaviour that has brought me to this state.
Go tell young and old to save themselves
From a similar plight, save each other, too
By grazing only where they have
Licence to graze. Out of range, is
Sure suicide. Except, of course, for the
Incidental victims like my poor wife –
Who suffer, who die, through the selfish
Careless, unthinking, stupid acts
Of those
They love.
Those who profess
To love them, dear.

If she could hear me
If she were still alive
My poor wife – the dear,
I'd tell her how sorry I am
How sorry I am
How sorry
Sorry
So so-ooOorryy!
Oh, my God!
GOD!
What have I done?
What have I done!

Please, take photographs!

Go to the nearest or cheapest electronic goods store
And there, buy cameras by the score.
Hurry! Go! Go! Go!
Then go home; gather your family and
Take photographs of them all
Especially the children; especially, the young,
Hurry! Take photos of them all
Before it is too late.

Take photographs of the children
Take photographs of them playing
Take photographs of them crying
Take photographs of them reading their best books
Or doing their chores – but –
Hurry! Hurry! Before it is too late.

Take photos of the children kneeling, busy at cat's cradle
Take photos of them naked and dancing in the rain
Take photos of them fast asleep in their cozy beds
Take photos of them in their school uniforms; their Sunday
    best, or ragged day dress.
But, please, hurry and take photos of the children,
Before it is too late
Before all the children are gone –
Before the promise that is their life
Is snuffed, easily as candlelight.

Your sons, so fearless, call sex with condoms
Eating candy with the wrapper on.
Perhaps their coffins they'll call castles
The ant and worm their company, slaves who do their
    bidding.

Please, take photographs, and tell the children why –
Take photos, before the young perish to the very last.
Take photographs! Take photographs, and put them on the
    walls
So the image of the dear face will forever live on.

I know, small comfort is a picture, your son or daughter
    gone.
Cold is a photo, from it comes not warmth nor smile nor
    hug.
A photo does not laugh; it will not go to the shop for you
Or be solace in your old age.

But, take photographs! Take photographs
So on birthdays and other days of remembrance
You can point to the picture on the wall and say –
Vusi would've been thirty today, perhaps with a
Young one and another on the way.

Take photos, take photos, before all the children are gone.
Before our tomorrow is no more –
Halved, at best, by the plague that comes with love;
Helped by the children who will not believe their
Dying – and men whose bones grew ever up,
The feet and inches, from the ground, sprouting.
Men who escaped the meaning of the passage of the years.
Who shot up, went to school – some;
But escaped the meaning of Social Responsibility.
To such souls, respect, respectable, respectability,
Are long dead; forget morality!
Doomed, despicable, craven images of humanity.

Please, hurry! Take photographs of all the children, now!
Take photos, for tomorrow they will be gone.
Take photos! Take photos of the children…
Children who will not see thirty.
Children who will never…grow…old.

Song of the orphan

Never to know, never to remember
The smile of a mother, at some silly thing
You and only you could have done.
Or the frown of a father, disapproving
Yes, strongly, but kindly still, kindly;
Never, but never, wavering in his love.

It's the hardest thing, to be an orphan
To never know, never remember
The days of sufficiency
When the world was complete.
Before the great plague came
And stole parents from children.
So the world remained forever after
A terribly wounded beast that never could heal;
Always at the ready to tear me apart.
Before this huge hole appeared, never to go away;
Never to fill, never to mend, never would the world
Be good again.
A lacuna where parents would have stood
The things they would have done, undone.
Never ever to be done!
And all that loving of children
Children who grow up bereft
Stricken, for having to go through life
Flying with broken wing.

Does anyone care, really care, what I do?
What heart sings at my success?
Who dies when I bleed, weeps because I'm ill?
Who loses sleep over my distress?
Catches fire,
Fords deep rivers,
Slays dragons,
So I can smile?

Poem to a brother

Language fails me
In our mother tongue, I'd ask
Ngowesingaphi ke lo?
Die hoeveelste een is die? I'd ask
In Afrikaans.
But in English
I'm plain tongue-tied
Trying to fashion a simple
Question that would elicit
The numeral, the number and order,
Telling me of your profane fecundity.

But, ma'an, I can't be
Bothered any more
Don't tell me, do not introduce me
To one more brat that has
Sprung from your unbridled loins.

I wince each time you
Open your buck-toothed mouth
Announce: Sisi, this is
My daughter/son! Beats me
How you keep track of
All these children's names when
You hardly see them
Never feed them
Seldom soothe their cares away.

Father, you call yourself!
Reckless sperm-spewer, I believe
A more apt epithet
For such brainless breeders;

Men who spit seed with the
Reckless abandon of dogs
Pissing against unnamed street
Poles or on random tufts of grass
Out on the unfeeling, unthinking veldt.

Noon, in the village

So still it is here,
In this place.
The sun at noon
Makes the rondavel
Cast no shade.

All is quiet; nothing moves.
And, as if by some secret signal,
Everyone's indoors.
The hens don't cackle,
The rooster doesn't crow.
God must be doing stocktaking
For His world to stand so still.

Foreign Aid

Foreign Aid
Comes to my country
Takes a U-turn
Goes back whence it came.

Foreign Aid
Big man President
Grins and grovels
Sells our coffee for a song
To get World Bank money.

Foreign Aid
Buys our country nothing
Gives our children less
This Dollar Democracy
Sure is expensive.

The sermon of the bones

If you are reading this note
That can only mean you live,
Your eyes have light;
Mine sealed in death.

Look then, you who live
Look, and do what I can't:
Make a difference in the world
Work day and night
Evil such as what brought me
To this place of death, to stop.

Look! Look and say ENOUGH!
Do not bequeath this ugly legacy
To your children and theirs,
Mine preceded me to the grave.

My prayer, as I lay myself down to die
Under the weeping African skies
Is that my bones speak in voice
Loud and clear. Loud and clear
For the men of Africa to heed.

Men of Africa, STOP the killing!
Men of Africa, STOP the killing!
Let Africa be home to love
Let understanding and respect thrive.
But, above all, let there be love
So that all things good may grow.

In this second between living
And dying
A blinding clarity is mine
Perfect understanding engulfs me
The root cause of Africa's wars
Of its famines, its endless strife:
Manifold cowardice.

Africa's people live in dire fear
Of Africa's governments, one and all.
An abomination, a travesty of justice:
It is the government who should live
In fear of the people; for the people
Are the real seat of power!

A war picture

For John Isaac

Sent to take photos
Record the carnage
Preserve it for posterity
He came back; heart hollowed.

There is no picture of the
Picture that undid him:
Baby suckling on breast
Mother – long, long dead.

Spectre of zero expectations

Six years, I'd left school
Six years, with nothing to show
All my little life, since I could count
There'd been an "Excellent!" or some such
To mark the harvest of the year's
Swotting over books and rubbing
Smarting hands, to soothe them
From the teacher's unforgiving lash.

But now, all I was, all I was
Expected to be was Mother!
I suppose it made some sense; when
Appended to that was the other epithet:
Wife! Thank God, he left.
Soon, misgiving flowered.
And, soon thereafter,
I bloomed!

A good woman

I said so yesterday, I'll say so tomorrow,
And I say so today: "I love you!
To me, you are life itself!"

Don't you understand?
Can't you see it, at all?
"I love you and always will!"

What I don't understand,
What I wish you'd let me know,
Is how do I fail you…and do so, so miserably?

What do you see in this one? What's the story, now?
You promised me – remember what you said, last time?
Darling, I'm so sorry…I'll never put you through this again!

Am I too short? Am I too tall? Or, is it my hair?
Shall I go into braids – or do you prefer a wig?
Shall I go blond? Blondes are much fun in bed, I'm told!

Is it my cooking? Have I been remiss in the kitchen?
Is it the flab – my midriff's no longer washboard hard!
I'll get implants – the dentures [yours and mine] do get in
    the way of play!

That Porsche you've been talking of –
I'll get a second job; part-time, of course! [there's cleaning
    and cooking to do!]
With the extra cash, we will well afford it!

I want to make you happy. You know, that is all I want!
Just tell me – please, tell me, what is it you want?

And I promise you, in next to no time, I'll be all that!

I'm a good woman; you say that yourself, you know!
Let me help you fight all this temptation
So we can live in peace from this day and on.

Just tell me, please, tell me…What in the world
Do you want? Don't you see, can't you see –
How much I do love you? I am a good woman.

But you turn a deaf ear to all my entreaties; I wonder why.
Clearly, do I see, all my selfless giving, my sacrifice and
My forgiving nature makes you sick to the core.

Know what? It makes me just as sick, if truth be known.
God, listen to me grovel at the stinking feet of a fool!
I'm a good woman; fool, you, for failing to see what's so
    plain to see.

But now, au revoir! I bequeath you to your newest love
I can think of no sweeter revenge than to let her keep you.
Unencumbered, I sally forth, my life to live with love at last.

I'm a good woman, and the best lover I have found!
All along I have known what great heart beats beneath this
    breast.
From now on, I will shower myself with love of self.

Never again will I waste my gifts on a confused mess of a
    man.
I know me and I love me just as I am.
And if in time, another should come my way,
That love will just have to stand in line
Behind my love of Me!

A mother remembers

See those mounds
At the far corner of the garden
Those are my children
Lying buried there.

Five in a row
Three girls, two boys
Such dear little ones. At least,
Now, they want for naught.

Your father never saw them
I have my memories
Every time he returned to
Plant one, one already gone.

Three weeks, each year he came
All the holiday due to such as him
He sent all the money he earned
But poverty was far stronger, bigger.

Yes, my heart is heavy; but I have
Memory of faces; which he has not.
He only has names that came in letters
Announcing births and passings.

Statement

I come to writing with no great learning
Except my life and the lives of the people
Of whom I am a part. For centuries,
Others have written about us
I write to change that
Instead of moaning about it.
I write so that children who look like me
In my country,
And my people, dispersed
Throughout the world,
May see someone who looks like them
Do this thing that has for so long
Not belonged to us.
I write so that the tale of the hunt
May be heard also, from the mouth of
The hunted; the hated of this world
For only then, will that story
Be anywhere near complete…

Why I write

I write because I cannot sing.
I write because I have lived
Have loved
Have seen what I have seen
Experienced what I have
Heard tales of terror, of torture
Witnessed the savagery of man

I write so that my children's
Children will also hear from me
So that the story of our past
And the story of the pass
Will be told also by those
Who lived and carried that shame

I write to leave footprints
To say: I have been
Have lived
This is who I am
Who I was
Who I have been
And so
I write.

Madam, please!

Three of us
Thinking ourselves
Grand and fine
And everything that is good
Went up the street to get lunch
Not *vetkoek* or chiproll today,
Oh, no! For such sophisticates
Fruit and milk, things all healthy.

Moreover, this being the time of
Black Consciousness
Good and proper did it seem
To support the brother at the corner.
So, to the fruit vendor we sauntered
Instead of the already far-too-fat-
cat shop owners on the
Main Road

Determined, the right thing to do,
Straight for the vendor made we;
Our money into our brother's
Hand to place; hang the white shops!
"Yes, Mama!" clapping his hands
The vendor hailed us; with the insult
Struck us dumb; rooted to the spot.

But, quickly, we recovered
Politically correct, took pity
On him, who'd had no education.
To remedy the deficiency, quietly we
Asked: Why do you always call us 'Mama'?
And here, let me frankly tell you
Fully did we a '*Merrem*' expect, no less.

Man nearly had a coronary
"What?" he shrieked, showing
All his toothless gums to boot.
"You think I can say 'Missus!' to you?"

And thus, began my education:
'*Merrem*', for white women, preserved
Missus, to women of his own class and hew
But me, poor me, if he deigned promote me
From kaffir, why, poor man already a rung
Had climbed. Decency made him refrain
From that. But, Lord, let me not expect too much.
Let me be reasonable: Mama is as far as he will go;
As far as he can go; already virtuous at the promotion
He has afforded the likes of me.
Why am I not grateful?
Because I want Merrem; right up there with the white woman.
Call me Madam, please. I am not your Mama!

Done did my bit

Today, I sat naked;
Eating yoghurt
From the tub

Some dropped and
Landed on the areola
Of my left breast.

At once, the picture
Brought to mind the tugging
Of a ravenous mouth.

So what if my tits
Hang till they kiss the
Navel, down south?

Damn, I deserve some
Respect for my part in
Nurturing life!

Picture perfect

Inspired by the photographs of UN photographer John Isaac

The picture says it all
You barely see her
Only head and shoulders peep
The rest of her deep in pit
Deep in the dry, dry pit.

Chucking out desert sand
Dug up with bare hands
Under the blazing sun; on and on
In vain pursuit of water,
She digs;
Digs
Till
She's
Totally out of sight
Deep in the hole
Looking for a drop of
Water.

Of a morning

I could have done my nails
Changed my hair style
Gone for a stroll in the mall
Instead, with these wounding visual cues
Men standing at street corners
Desperate bodies emaciated
Haunted-animal look in eye,
I wrote a poem on hunger.

The revolution within

'Damn this blight!'
The body said.
The right eye's gone bad on me.
I will not have it! I'm sure
I am much better without.

Have you ever?
With the eye, I thought
All that was done.
What's this now?
What's with the accursed leg?

Why then, I will show it,
Yes, I will!
Where's my well-sharpened knife?
Or, should I a scapel get?
Rid myself of this new affront?
This abomination? This…this…this
Ungrateful limb that's turned against me?

And so the besieged body went
Hacking away, butchering itself
With sharp tongue, it slashed itself,
Angrily flagellated each part
That Time's wear and tear entertained.

Away it flayed and sliced, speared and lanced
Bit and clawed and kicked and butted
Forgetting the very simple fact:
Indivisible, one and ever one
Is this body-corporate we call society.

Freedom

I will be free
But long lines once
Every five years or so
Are not my goal.

I know. I know.
For this, thousands died.
My hat I humbly doff
For this sacred sacrifice.

I will be free. Yes, I will be free,
From hunger and joblessness
From living in fire traps
Overrepresentation in all
Diseases of chance
From early graves for my
Little ones; toothlessness
For my aged mothers;
Blind-alley education;
Inescapable welfare
Sapping what little remains
Of my self-respect.

I will be free! Oh, yes, I will be free
From fear   From hunger   From want
Of every kind. From crunching debt;
Diminishing dreams. From shrinking
Life path – forth shall I burst
Brimming with zest – ready and eager
Tall to stand. Taller still to stretch
Till by sheer force of unquenchable will
Yesterday's shadow, down the cliff I drive

Yesterday's sorrow, in deepest sea I drown
To arise insistent
Unpushdownable as the rising morn
I will be free
I will be free!
Oh, yes! Yes!
I will be free!

Hands off my brain!

Lure me not into your
Black Studies Department
Where I will learn of your
Interpretation of the meaning
Of my existence.

Not so soon. Not so soon.
Not when I can still smell
My blood on your knuckles.
Lure me not into your fine
Institutions.

The knowledge of my hurt;
The bleedings from the beatings
The losses, the deaths, the decay
Of my institutions – all these sorrows
Are branded deep in my psyche.

You trampled on my dreams;
Sowed sorrow in my soul;
Tore my whole world to shreds.
But my spirit has survived;
And I will teach you
The meaning of my existence.

Lure me not into your fine institutions;
My very living is university par excellence.
I have overcome slavery, apartheid, and wholesale
Plunder at your hand. Let me tell the story –
I, who have lived it, know it best.

Brother, wait!

Do not, for a minute, believe the hype;
The revolution is far from over.
You still have a role to play
Not on the battlefield but in your
Home and in your community.

Perhaps, the greatest contribution
You can make is: Love the mother
Of your children. Love her!

The revolution is far from over;
Rest not on your laurels, let not your
Guard down. Our numbers are our
Greatest strength. Killing a sister helps
The other side.

Not guns against the enemy
But love among ourselves
Today, this is the weapon black people
Everywhere must wield:
Love!
Love of self
In total community!

Unseen wounds

No name
No headstone
No grave
You never lived.

Nine months, though,
You did
Inside my womb.

You smiled
You tossed
You fed
Inside my womb

My womb
Arid desert
Had naught to give
You persevered.

You fought for the right
To be born and see the light
To live
To grow.

My womb
Microcosm of my world
Slowly executed you
Brave frail warrior.

We knit your bones
From fibre of my teeth
Nine months, side by side
Valiantly we fought.

I have no teeth
You have no name
There is no headstone
No grave.

To lovers past

Like the tender shoot of young corn
All I ever needed was the water of your smile
And the strong, sure sun of your soul.
I came into the world already armed
With the impetus to become, to be.
I am the rich soil, the good earth
The loam of everlasting, never-ending time
The essence of all living. I am life!
All I ever needed, was the water of
Your smile.

The taste of change

Mandela in jail
No milk in my bottle
Mother at work
I hungry

De Klerk free Mandela
No milk in my bottle
Father at work
I sick

Mandela meet De Klerk
People clap and dance
Rain come through my roof
I cold

Change on every lip
Father mother work
Me and thousand others
We die.

A wish

Grow, good things, grow!
Grow and fill the land
Mushroom and bloom and spread
Infect us all.
Grow and infest us all
Drive out all the evil which abounds
Grow here and there and everywhere
Sprout and spread; thicken and quicken
Spread far and wide like the plague.

A promise

We shall live to be old
You and I.
And we will tell stories
Of our living, our loving –
The dreams of our youth
And the folly of our old age
The nightmares we witnessed
Parading around pretending
To be reality…

The village

Somehow it seems preordained
This symmetry of round huts
Muted shades of mud gray
And thatch; easy sameness
Set against soft rounded hills
Green-gray-brown mountains
All exuding an air of
Profound serenity.

Our thanks

The highest form of thanks
Our highest tribute to Nature
For her boundless bounty
Is to leave her seeming
As though we have not been.

Village time

There is time in the village.
Time for day's chores
Is ordered; and all know
When to do what; just as though
A day were a season, complete.

There is time in the village.
Where few have watches,
God's sun watches over all
It is the watch of all in the village
By the rise and setting of that sun
The village orders its day.

There is time in the village.
It sets the pace by which people live;
Rushing and loudness foreign,
Chaos clashes with mud living,
Swift movement is foreign
Like loud voices unless called for
In joy, ululation; in death, keening.
But of an ordinary day, as the sun
Journeys across broad blue sky
Seemingly effortless are the ways
Of village folk; people of soft-spoken
Words; sustained tenderness shrouded
In lingering shy smiles that reach deep into eye.

Other poetry titles by Modjaji Books

Fourth Child
by Megan Hall

Life in Translation
by Azila Talit Reisenberger

Burnt Offering
by Joan Metelerkamp

Oleander
by Fiona Zerbst

Strange Fruit
by Helen Moffett

Invisible Earthquake
A Women's Journal Through Stillbirth
(Poetic Memoir)
by Malika Ndlovu

http://modjaji.book.co.za